PIGS™

VOLUME ONE:

HELLO, CRUEL WORLD

IMAGE COMICS, INC.
Robert Kirkman - chief operating officer
Erik Larsen - chief financial officer
Todd McFarlane - president
Marc Silvestri - chief executive officer
Jim Valentino - vice-president

Eric Stephenson - publisher
Todd Martinez - sales & licensing coordinator
Jennifer de Guzman - pr & marketing coordinator
Branwyn Bigglestone - accounts manager
Emily Miller - administrative assistant
Jamie Parreno - marketing assistant
Sarah deLaine - events coordinator
Kevin Yuen - digital rights coordinator
Tyler Shainline - production manager
Drew Gill - art director
Jonathan Chan - senior production artist
Monica Garcia - production artist
Vincent Kukua - production artist
Jana Cook - production artist
www.imagecomics.com

image

PIGS VOL. 1: HELLO, CRUEL WORLD. First Printing. February 2012. Published by Image Comics, Inc. Office of publication: 2134 Allston Way, 2nd Floor, Berkeley, CA 94704. For information regarding the CPSIA on this printed material call: 203-595-3636 and provide reference # EAST – 421588. International Rights Representative: Christine Meyer — christine@gfloystudio.com. ISBN: 978-1-60706-512-8. Printed in the United States.

NATE COSBY & BEN McCOOL
WRITERS

BRENO TAMURA
WITH **WILL SLINEY**
ARTISTS

CHRIS SOTOMAYOR
WITH **DONNA GREGORY**
COLOR ARTISTS

RUS WOOTON
LETTERING & DESIGN

COVERS BY
JOCK
DECLAN SHALVEY & JORDIE BELLAIRE
FRANCESCO FRANCAVILLA
AMANDA CONNER & PAUL MOUNTS
BECKY CLOONAN

SPECIAL THANKS TO
JOE PRADO & BECKY CLOONAN

'PIGS' CREATED BY NATE COSBY & BEN McCOOL

OUR FATHERS' WARS

It was easy in the old days. We were the good guys and they were the bad guys. Went without saying, right? If you're not with us, you're against us! And so, secure in our own moral superiority, we could happily relax to the vicarious thrill of watching our fictional heroes unleash seven shades of unholy shit upon them.

"Them" being Commies, terrorists, dictators, whoever. It made life nice and easy for writers of thrillers and action movies, having this seemingly endless stream of off-the-shelf bad guys to slot into the narrative.

But gradually, the world got complicated on us. Or maybe, just maybe, we finally wised up, and realized it had always had been that way...

The Cold War ended, and it turned out the Russians aren't the monsters we'd always made them out to be. Those evil dictators in South America and the Middle East turned out to have been propped up by our own governments... as long as they toed the company line.

The old moral absolutes don't hold up any more. Where once we saw One Nation Under God versus the Axis of Evil, now we see a dizzyingly complex global web of mutual interdependencies, compromises, payoffs and hypocrisies.

It's a Wikileaks world now; one in which we've been forced to challenge our cozy assumptions. We look to ourselves, ashamed of our complicity and hypocrisy. Maybe the "bad guys" are just ordinary people like us. Maybe they got lied to, just like us...

Because really, that's what it all comes down to - whether we believe what we're told by those in power. Maybe we used to. But we're sick and tired of being lied to, from WMDs to Wall Street. So who are you gonna believe? Truth is you have to play smart, stay informed, and make up your own mind. Follow your own moral compass. And keep your Bullshit Radar set to max.

As the world changes, we need to change with it. It's the forces of the past that try to hold us back - because those who benefited most from the status quo are those with the most to lose.

Which brings us to PIGS.

What Nate Cosby, Ben McCool and Breno Tamura have done is distil this cross-generational political friction into a brilliantly nasty, non-linear narrative. Just like us, Havana, Victor, Ekatarina, Aleksandr and Felix were raised with moral absolutes. Just like us, they believe themselves to be the good guys. And just like us, they're starting to wonder if they've been fed a serious line of horseshit...

Will they reject the ideologies they were raised with, and adapt to a changing world? Mutate and survive? Or will they carry on unquestioningly fighting their fathers' wars for them?

Will we...?

PIGS
JORDIE 2011

MIAMI.
NOW.

SOMETHIN'...

SIR, MIGHT HAVE MOVEMENT OFF THE PORT BOW.
ALL LIGHTS OFF THE PORT BOW.
U.S. COAST

CAAAAAAAAAAAALLLLM

THEY DON'T SEE US.
CALM.

WASHINGTON, D.C.
SOON.
I WILL HAVE A CUP OF WATER.
BITCH, I DON'T THINK YOU UNDERSTAND WHAT THE FUCK IS HAPPENING.
TEA, IF YOU HAVE IT.

ANSWER MY FUCKING QUESTION.
"BITCH, I DON'T THINK YOU UNDERSTAND WHAT THE FUCK IS HAPPENING" IS NOT A QUESTION.
I REPEAT:
CAN YOU VERIFY THE EXISTENCE OF A KGB SLEEPER CELL PLACED INSIDE CUBA IN 1962?
I DON'T KNOW WHAT YOU ASK.
I THINK YOU DO.
THINK INCORRECTLY ALL YOU LIKE.

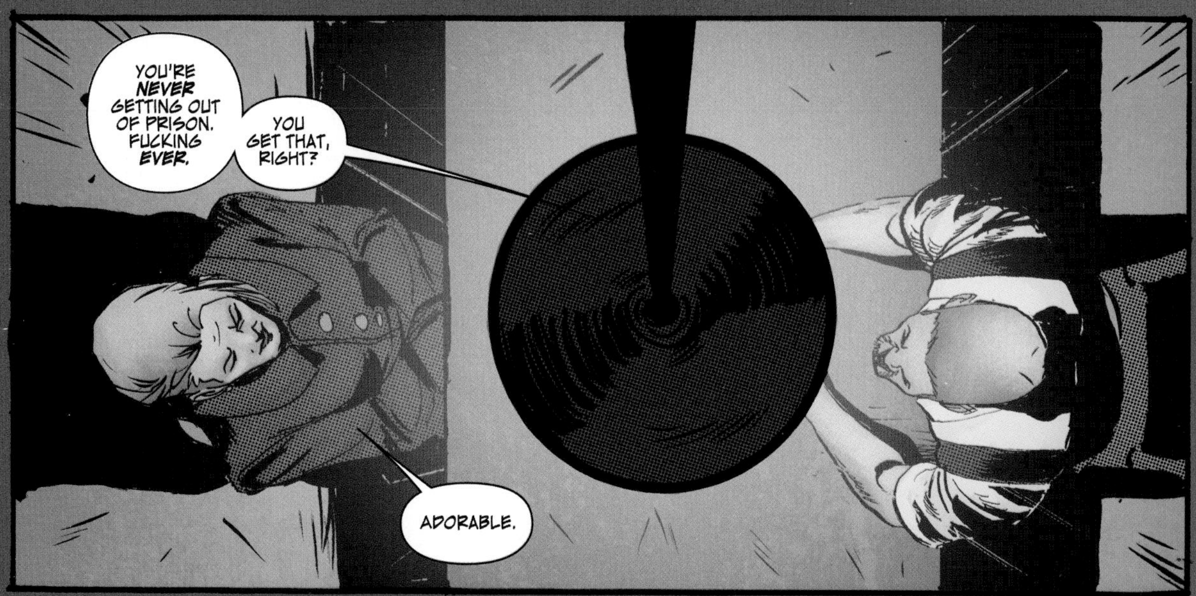
YOU'RE NEVER GETTING OUT OF PRISON. FUCKING EVER.
YOU GET THAT, RIGHT?
ADORABLE.

YOU LOWER YOUR VOICE AN OCTAVE. TO SOUND TOUGH.
YOUR BODY LANGUAGE IS AGGRESSIVE. TO INTIMIDATE.
AND YOU SAY "FUCK." BECAUSE... YOU THINK A WOMAN WILL FEAR THE WORD?

THE INFORMATION YOU PRESENT, AND WHAT YOU HOPE FOR IN RETURN... YOU WASTE TIME.
YOU ATTEMPT TO FRIGHTEN AN OLD WOMAN INTO ADMITTING THINGS THAT ARE NOT TRUE.

YOU ASK ME OF 1962? OF THE KBG? THESE ARE OLD THINGS.
YOU SPEAK OF OLD MEN.

ALL OF THE OLD MEN I KNEW ARE DEAD.
CUBA. EARLIER.

!!
ALEJANDRO--!

I'M SO SORRY, VIDLEN! I ONLY TOOK MY EYE OFF HIM FOR A SECOND!
IT'S FINE, MS. BAPTISTA-- HE'S QUITE THE BUNDLE OF ENERGY!

GAHK
AHHU
AUGH

NAHHGHF!
NUH FUH
MMNF
TOMA
GUHH
felizidades a mi esposa querida
GDBY
HNNT
WE ARE ALL HEARTBROKEN.

VIDLEN WAS A GREAT MAN. THE HEART OF US.

HE LOVED EVERY ONE OF YOU, AS IF YOU WERE HIS SONS AND DAUGHTERS.
MOURN HIM, CHERISH THE THOUGHT OF HIM. AND REMEMBER WHAT I SAY NEXT IS WHAT HE WOULD ASK... IF I WERE IN THE GROUND INSTEAD OF HIM.

DO ANY OF YOU SUSPECT MURDER?

NO.
NO.
NO.
HAVANA, HAVE YOU ANALYZED THE MEDICAL REPORT?
YES, MAMA...
...HEART ATTACK. NO DRUGS OTHER THAN HIS NORMAL MEDICATIONS.
PIE-1372
NATURAL CAUSES.

IS ANYONE BEING FOLLOWED? NOTICED ANYTHING PECULIAR?
ARE THERE NEW PEOPLE WORKING AT YOUR JOBS?

NO.
NO.
NO.

ALL RIGHT.
VIKTOR.

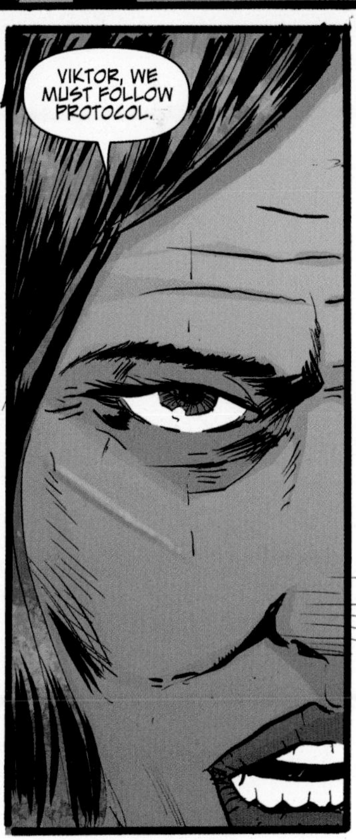
VIKTOR, WE MUST FOLLOW PROTOCOL.

I'VE SEARCHED THE HOUSE. IT'S CLEAN.

I AM SURE. BUT IT IS YOUR **FATHER'S** HOUSE. YOU MAY HAVE MISSED SOMETHING.

IT'S **MY** HOUSE NOW.

HAVANA WILL NOT BOTHER ANY--
I DON'T WANT THAT **WHORE** TOUCHING EVERYTHING I OWN!
HEY NOW--
WE KNOW HOW SHE **"OBTAINED"** THE MEDICAL RECORDS! I BET SHE **FUCKED** THE CORONER IN THE SAME ROOM WITH PAPA'S BODY!
DUDE! THAT'S NOT--
VIKTOR.

YOUR FATHER HAS PASSED. YOUR MIND IS *TANGLED.*
BUT IF YOU CALL MY DAUGHTER A WHORE IN MY PRESENCE EVER AGAIN...
I WILL SLIT YOUR THROAT.

EKATARINA.
SEARCH THE HOUSE. BE VERY CAREFUL NOT TO DISTURB ANYTHING.
YES, MAMA.

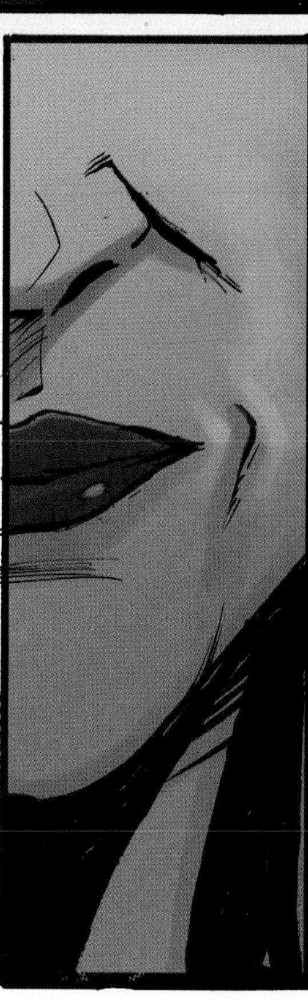

BAY OF PIGS?
YES.
IS THAT WHERE THEY MAKE BACON?
NO.
BECAUSE I AM A HUGE FAN OF BACON.

1961, THE CIA TRAINS UP A BUNCHA CUBAN EXILES AND DROPS THEM OFF AT THE BAHIA DE COCHIOS, OR "BAY OF PIGS."
THEY'RE SUPPOSED TO OVERTHROW CASTRO.
IT GOES SPECTACULARLY SHITTY.

PISSES CASTRO OFF SO BAD THAT IN 1962, HE LETS MOTHER RUSSIA PUT HUGE-ASS MISSILES IN CUBA, POINTED AT AMERICA.

THE SOVIETS SEND MISSILES, MILITARY, WEAPON INSTALLATION SPECIALISTS, AND AN AGRICULTURAL DELEGATION.

AN AGRICULTURAL DELEGATION.
WHY DID THE SOVIETS SEND A DELEGATION OF AGRICULTURISTS TO CUBA IN 1962?
IT IS EVERY RUSSIAN'S DREAM TO SEE A COCONUT.
FEW MONTHS GO BY, KENNEDY AND KHRUSHCHEV WORK IT OUT. THE MISSILES, WEAPON GUYS, MILITARY... THEY GET ON BOATS'N GO HOME.
KNOW WHO DOESN'T GET ON A BOAT...?
GILLIGAN?
THE AGRICULTURAL DELEGATION.
NO INTELLIGENCE ON THEM LEAVING CUBA.

THEY COULD STILL BE THERE, COULDN'T THEY?

LITERALLY *ANYTHING* IS POSSIBLE.

YEAH.
LITERALLY *ANYTHING.*
HE WOULD HAVE HATED THESE FLOWERS.
YEAH. HE ONLY LIKED RED LOTUSES.

MAMA, GO HOME.
WHAT?

I WANT TO TALK TO PAPA ALONE. CAN I DO THAT?

OF COURSE.

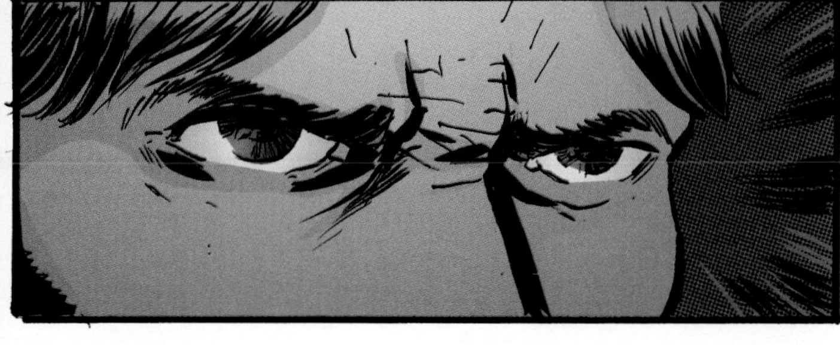

WHO THE FUCK...

HIH--
NUAHH--!
GAAK
GRFF
NRRG
TIME TO DIE FOR YOUR COUNTRY, BOY.

WHAT DID HE SAY? *EXACTLY?*
YOU KNOW WHAT HE SAID.

HE SAID THE WORDS, ALEK.
THE REAL WORDS.

WE'VE WAITED TO HEAR THEM OUR *WHOLE LIVES.*

WE GET TO AMERICA.
DON'T GET SEEN, DON'T GET CAUGHT.
CALM.

AND WHEN WE GET THERE, BEFORE WE BEGIN THE MISSION... BEFORE DOING WHAT WE WERE *BORN* TO DO...

...WE GO GET THE ***WHITE RUSSIAN.***

YOU THINK WE'RE FISHING.
DUMBASS COPS, DON'T KNOW SHIT. HOPING YOU TRIP UP'N GIVE US SOMETHING.
AIN'T TRUE.
WE GOT HARD EVIDENCE SAYS YOU KNOW LOTS.

THERE ARE SO MANY LIVES AT STAKE.
SO PLEASE, FOR THE LOVE OF GOD, HELP US OUT A LITTLE HERE.

NO THANK YOU.
GOD MOTHER FUCKING DAMMIT! I SWEAR TO--

STOP.
I'M NOT PLAYING COLD WAR WITH THIS FUCKING CUNT!

HOW IN THE FUCK ARE KGB AGENTS THAT'RE SUPPOSED TO BE SEVENTY RIPPING THE ENTIRE FUCKING COUNTRY APART...

...AND WHERE THE FUCK IS THE REST OF THE PRESIDENT?!
CONTINUED...

FRAN CAVIL LA F.11
PIGS

CUBA. 1991.

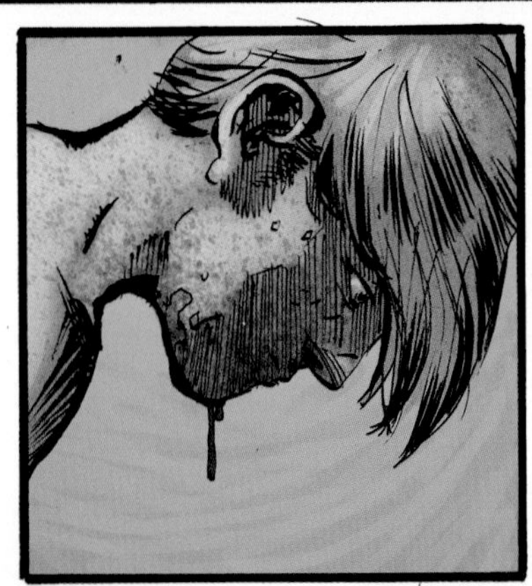

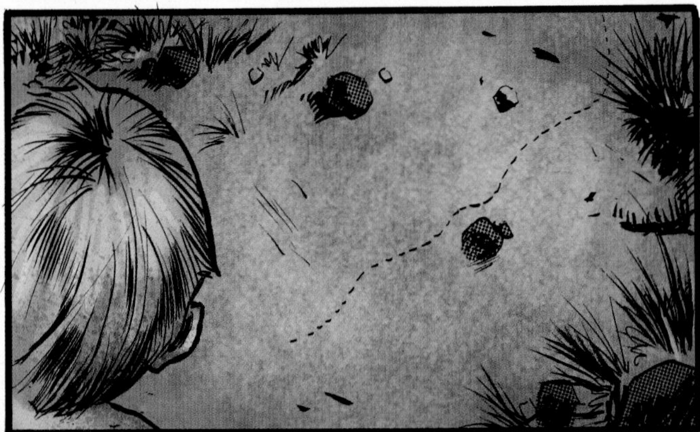

YOU DON'T NEED TO KNOW. THAT'S NOT THE POINT.

X IS A THING THAT REPRESENTS SOMETHING YOU DON'T NEED TO KNOW.

MIAMI. NOW.
SO YOU'VE GOT 8X - 4 = 12. HOW DO YOU START?
I'M NEVER GONNA USE THIS IN REAL LIFE, RIGHT?
NOPE.
BUT IF YOU DON'T LEARN IT NOW, YOU FAIL MATH.
THEN YOU REPEAT THE THIRD GRADE.

THEN YOU'RE STUCK IN A CLASS WITH BOYS A FOOT SHORTER THAN YOU THAT'LL YANK ON YOUR PONYTAIL.

DING-DONG
DO WE WANT THAT?
...NO.

SO WE'RE LEARNING MATH?
...YEAH.

BEHOLD:
THE WHITE RUSSIAN.
PRODIGAL
NATE COSBY & BEN McCOOL • WRITERS
BRENO TAMURA • ARTIST
CHRIS SOTOMAYOR • COLORIST
RUS WOOTON • LETTERER/DESIGNER
FRANCESCO FRANCAVILLA • COVER ARTIST
SPECIAL THANKS TO BECKY CLOONAN & JOE PRADO

ALEK.
EKAT...

SARAH?
WE HAVE COMPANY.
OH. OH MY GOD.

WHAT ARE YOU--! OH MY GOD!

HOW ARE YOU ALL HERE?!
SORRY, JUST GOT OFF A BOAT. I PROBABLY STINK....

HOW'D YOU DO IT? DID YOU STOW AWAY, OR--
THEY JUST GOT OUT OF THE WATER, SARAH.

MAYBE THEY NEED TO RELAX A SECOND? EAT?
OF COURSE! I HAVE CALDOSA AND RICE AND...

LET'S DO A LITTLE OF EVERYTHING.
RIGHT, YES. I HOPE THERE'S ENOUGH...DIDN'T EXPECT TO FEED AN ARMY TONIGHT!

COME ON, ADRIANA!
WHO ARE THEY, MOMMY?

WE'VE COME FOR OUR ONE-MAN ARMY, FELIX...
HAVE YOU BEEN PREPARING FOR WAR?

HNN...
HNR...

HNN

P-PLEASE

YOU ARE NOT REQUIRED TO ENJOY THE PAIN.

BUT YOU WILL BECOME ACCUSTOMED TO IT.

PLINK
PLINK
PLINK
PLINKPLINKPLINK
HOW DO YOU KNOW THIS IS LEGITIMATE?
HE TOLD VIKTOR THE WORDS. THE *REAL WORDS.*

HE COULD'VE BEEN A FAKE.

HE KNEW ABOUT THE *NUMBERS.*

PLINK
PLINK
PLINK

FUCK.

PLINK
PLINK
PLINK

AND SO YOU ALL CONTINUED YOUR TRAINING?
OF COURSE.

I DIDN'T.

OF COURSE.

PLINK PLINK
PLINK
PLINK

YOU CAN'T HONESTLY THINK I'M GOING WITH YOU.
PERSONAL STUFF OUT THE WINDOW, MAN. MISSION COMES FIRST.
IT'S NOT MY MISSION.
IT'S WHAT WE WERE BORN FOR.

WE'RE NOT DOGS, ALEK. WE DON'T HAVE MASTERS.
YOU'VE COME TO MY HOME, UNANNOUNCED, BRINGING WITH YOU SHIT I'VE SPENT TEN YEARS TRYING TO FORGET.

PLINK
PLINK
PLINK

THEY RAISED US TO BE BAD PEOPLE. WE DON'T HAVE TO BE THAT.
WE HAVE A CHOICE.

PLNXKLWK

I MADE MY CHOICE.
I'M NOT WHO I WAS. I'M TRYING TO BE BETTER.
YOU THINK YOU'RE AMERICAN?

I'M NOT CUBAN, AND I'M SURE AS SHIT NOT FUCKING RUSSIAN.
WE'RE BASTARDS FROM NOWHERE. ALL OF US.

WE'RE NOT SUPPOSED TO EXIST.

BUT WE DO, AND I'M MAKING THE MOST OF IT. THAT MEANS BEING THERE FOR MY WIFE AND DAUGHTER.
NOT KILLING INNOCENTS BECAUSE GHOSTS TOLD US TO.
YOU'LL GIVE US YOUR NUMBERS?
I WILL.

THEN WE'LL LEAVE, AND WISH YOU WELL.

STAY THE NIGHT. PLEASE.
IT'D MEAN A LOT TO SARAH.

THANK YOU, FELIX.
OF COURSE WE'LL STAY.

PLINK
PLINK
PLINK
PLINK

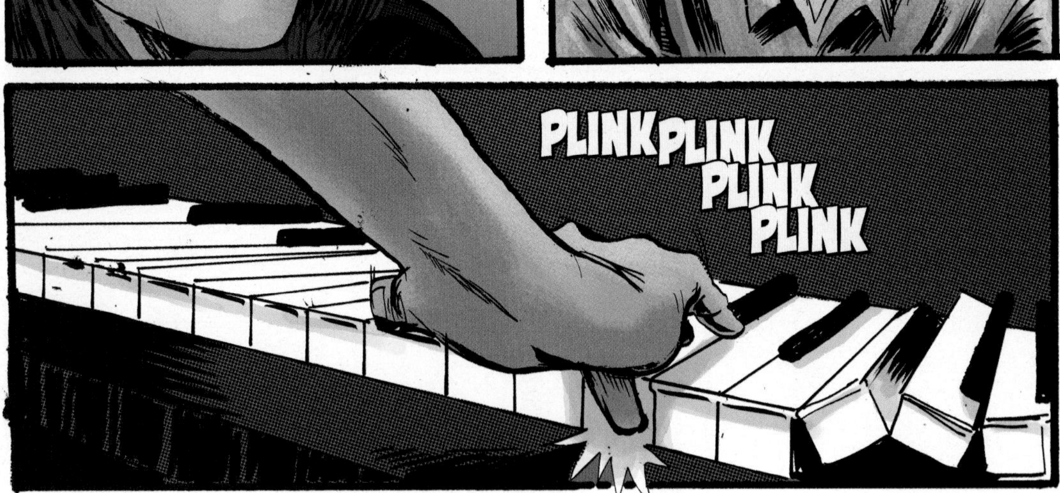
PLINK PLINK PLINK PLINK

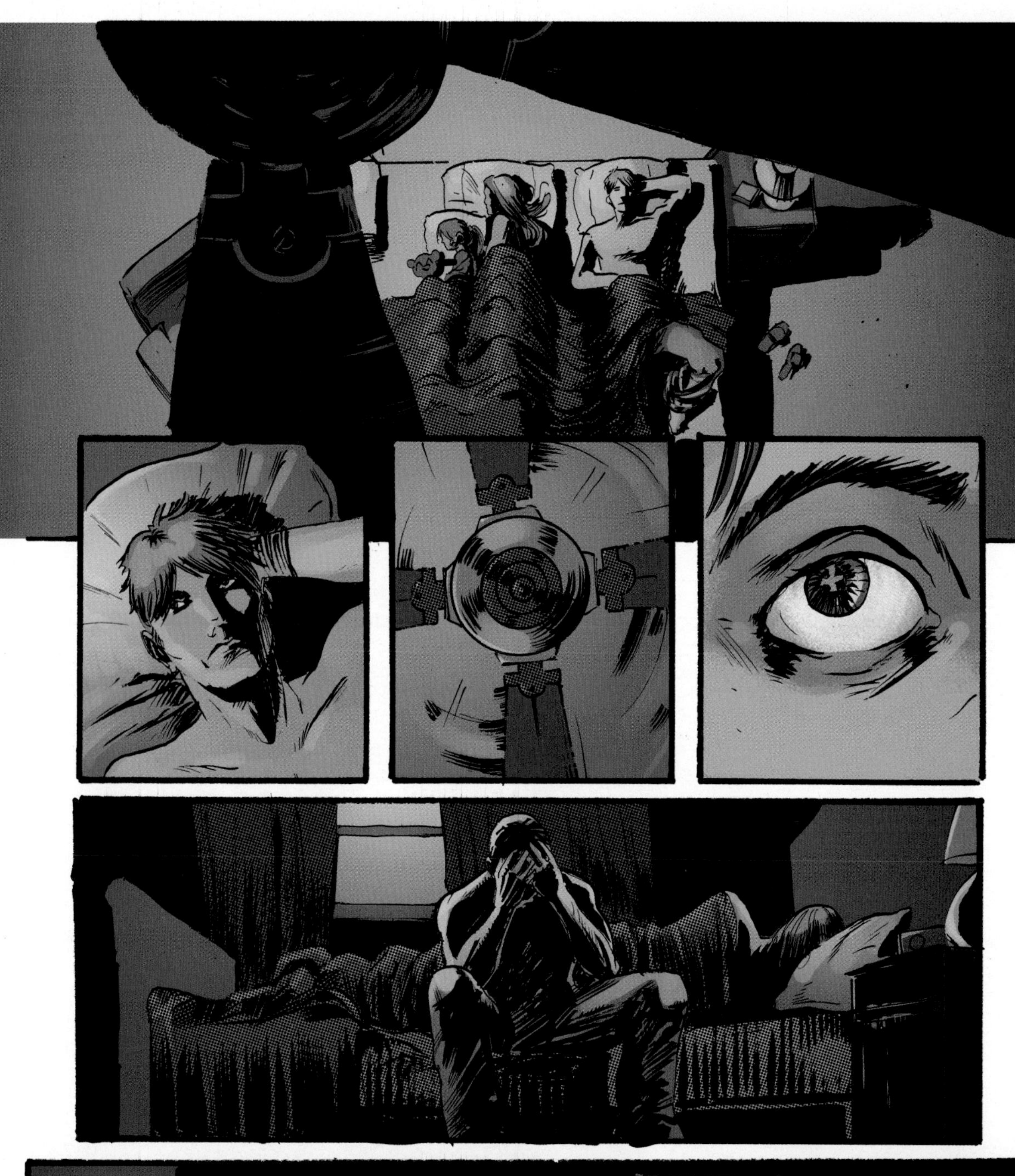

TCK

GAAK
HRN
HRG
HRN

UK
YOU'LL COME WITH US.
GRK...HH...
YOU'LL COME WITH US...
KUH
OR YOUR BITCHES ARE DEAD.
HH
HHU
NNH

HOW LONG?
AT LEAST A MONTH. MAYBE MORE.
BUT WHAT DO THEY NEED YOU FOR?
PLEASE DON'T ASK ME.
I WON'T LIE TO YOU. BUT PLEASE DON'T ASK.
I-I...
I JUST DON'T UNDERSTAND, FELIX. AND WHAT HAPPENED TO YOUR HEAD? DID--
SARAH.
IT'S ALL GOING TO BE JUST FINE. YOU'LL SEE.
SEE YOU SOON, PRINCESS.

MY STRENGTH, ALL I AM, IS YOURS.
I LOVE YOU SO MUCH.

CLICK!
CLICK!
NN
HOW DO YOU FEEL, FELIX?
STRONGER

AND WHAT WILL YOU DO WITH YOUR STRENGTH?

IT IS NOT *MY* STRENGTH. IT BELONGS TO THE ***MOTHERLAND.***

COME.

YOUR MOTHER WILL HAVE DINNER READY SOON.
YES, PAPA.
CONTINUED

CONNER
MOUNTS

NOW.
KANSAS CITY, KANSAS.
EXIT

ANY TROUBLE?

IT WENT FINE.
RUGSTORE

NORTH
I-70 W
HOW MUCH DID IT COST?
NOTHING.

KANSAS GUN-TRADER
GUNS SALE
10% OFF
GUNS SALE
BULLETS 30% OFF

IT WENT FINE.
"ROCKY"
NATE COSBY & BEN MCCOOL · WRITERS
BRENO TAMURA · ARTIST
CHRIS SOTOMAYOR · COLOR ARTIST
RUS WOOTON · LETTERER & PRODUCTION
AMANDA CONNER & PAUL MOUNTS · COVER
SPECIAL THANKS TO JOE PRADO & BECKY CLOONAN

CUBA. 1992.
HUH
HUH
HUH
HRRAAA

NRRRSH

PREDICTABLE. SLUGGISH.
NOT HOW FELIX WAS TAUGHT TO FIGHT.

UAACHH
GUHH--!
BETTER.
MNAA

BLRRP

GBRRAAAA

GAAAAAK

HNNNN
UUUUMPH

MUH GUH
WHHHUU

ALEK, ARE YOU--
AGAIN.
BUT...
AGAIN.

NOW.
CASTLE ROCK, COLORADO.

THE MOUNTAINS ARE SO PRETTY.

HAVE YOU BEEN HERE BEFORE?
WE TOOK ADRIANA TO DISNEYWORLD WHEN SHE WAS SEVEN.

THAT'S THE ONLY TIME I LEFT MIAMI.

LADY L MOTEL
KLIK
WE GET A NUMBER FROM ROCKY COLLINS.
THAT'S ALL HE SAID?

YEAH. "GET THE TWELVE DIGIT CODE FROM ROCKY COLLINS AT 650 BRUSH CREEK ROAD."

GREAT. THIS IS *GREAT.*

GO TO COLORADO AND GET A NUMBER FROM A GUY WE'VE NEVER HEARD OF.
HE'S A SENATOR FROM UTAH.

WHAT?
ROCKY COLLINS IS A U.S. SENATOR FROM UTAH, *"VACATIONING"* IN ASPEN.

HE'S BEING INVESTIGATED FOR...SOMETHING ABOUT LAND AND ZONING RIGHTS. SO HE'S LAYING LOW HERE.

AT 650 BRUSH CREEK ROAD.

THIS IS THE MISSION? VIKTOR GETS A CALL FROM WHOEVER-THE-FUCK, EKAT CHECKS GOOGLE, WE GO IN GUNS BLAZING?

THIS IS FUCKING RIDICULOUS.

YOU'D PREFER A LENGTHY DOSSIER? HM? A SERIES OF MEETINGS THAT COVER EVERY MINUTE DETAIL OVER AND OVER AND OVER?
THE MITH of

RUSSIA HAS GIVEN US A NAME, AN ADDRESS, AND A GOAL.
WE HAVE EVERYTHING WE NEED.
RUSSIA.

RUSSIA NEVER GAVE ME SHIT.

CUBA. 1992.
...JUST SAYING WE SHOULD KEEP AN EYE ON HIM. I'VE SEEN HIM THREE OUT OF THE LAST FOUR TIMES I'VE BEEN TO THE MARKET.
MAYBE HE FANCIES YOU.
IF YOU SEE HIM AGAIN, REMEMBER AND REPORT.
ANYTHING ELSE?
WE ARE ADJOUR--
I WANT...
...I WANTED TO TALK ABOUT SOMETHING.
I'M A LITTLE CONCERNED... ABOUT THE CHILDREN.

I WATCHED FELIX AND ALEKSANDR SPAR TODAY...THEY ARE AMAZING.
SOLDIERS. **WARRIORS.** THEY GAVE THEIR ENTIRE SELVES TO THE EXERCISE.
BUT THE FIRE INSIDE THEM...THE FIRE **WE** HAVE FANNED...I WORRY IT WILL CONSUME THEM.
ARE WE PRESSURING THE COAL TOO MUCH TO MAKE OUR DIAMONDS? WE ARE SO SINGLE-MINDEDLY DETERMINED TO CREATE AN ARMY, BUT ARE WE FORGETTING THAT THEY SHOULD BE ALLOWED TO LIVE FOR THEMSELVES?
ARE WE STUNTING THEIR GROWTH BY AGING THEM TOO QUICKLY?

NUAA!!

YOU PATHETIC FUCK.
YOU WILL REMEMBER YOURSELF. YOU WILL REMEMBER WHY WE ARE HERE.
I WOULD KILL YOU. I WOULD KILL EVERY ONE OF YOU! IF IT WAS FOR THE GOOD OF THE MISSION. OF OUR CAUSE. OF WHAT IS RIGHT.

OLEG.

LISTEN, I--
YOU WILL NEVER DEFY ME, YURI.
OR I WILL SPEND TWO YEARS KILLING YOU. ONE YEAR DESTROYING YOUR MIND, THE OTHER CHOPPING YOUR BODY INTO TINY FUCKING BITS.

DO YOU UNDERSTAND ME, YOU TRAITOROUS PIECE OF DOGSHIT!? DO YOU FUCKING COMPREHEND!?

ANSWER!

Y-YES, OLEG.

I COMPREHEND.

NOW.
...SWEAR TO GOD, MAN, THE BITCH IS CRAZY. PULLS MY HAIR, BITES MY FACE, SCRATCHES MY BACK TO SHIT.
LOVES THE SIGHT OF BLOOD AND EVERYTHING.
JESUS. I COULD USE SOME OF THAT RIGHT NOW.
AIN'T HAD A WOMAN NEAR MY JUNK IN MONTHS.

NO EXCITEMENT IN MY LIFE, MAN.

GAAH--!
POK

BAAM
WHAT--?
HOLD IT, MOTHERFUCKERS! YOU ARE FUCKING DEAD!
URK
HUH?

LOOK, OVER THERE! THERE'RE MORE OF THEM!
POK
FUCK.
TRANQUILIZERS.
WHEN I GET MY HANDS ON THAT FUCKING COWARD--

HRRG
MMMFAA
ACK

INSIDE.
UH
UH
UH
YEAHYEAHYEAH
OH GOD THAT'S IT YEAH...
WH-WHO THE FUCK--
H-HUH...?
NO NO, DON'T LET ME DISTRACT YOU, ROCKY--

FINISH UP.
CONTINUED...

AHUH AHUH AHUH

I WANT TO HELP I WANT TO HELP I'LL GIVE YOU ANYTHING IF I KNEW I FUCKING SWEAR TO GOD I WOULD

SCHLNKK
GLYAAAAAAAA!!!!!!

OH G- OH GOD OH MY GOD MMF
PLEASE
PROBLEM IS, ROCKY...

I DON'T BELIEVE YOU.
UMF HUUUUGH
TAKE IT OUT PLEASE TAKE IT
"SIXTEEN"
NATE COSBY & BEN MCCOOL - STORY
BRENO TAMURA - ARTIST
WILL SLINEY - FLASHBACK ARTIST
CHRIS SOTOMAYOR &
DONNA GREGORY - COLOR ARTISTS
RUS WOOTON - LETTERING & DESIGN
BECKY CLOONAN - COVER ARTIST
SPECIAL THANKS TO JOE PRADO & BECKY CLOONAN
'PIGS' CREATED BY NATE COSBY & BEN MCCOOL

NO PROBLEM, ROCKY...
NYAAAAAAAAAAAAAAAAAAAAAAAAAAAAAAAA
YOU FUCKING PUSSY.

TRANQUILIZERS?
THERE WAS NO NEED FOR THE GUARDS TO DIE.

IT MADE SENSE TO--
WE ARE TRAINED TO TORTURE AND KILL, FELIX. WE DO NOT POLITELY WALK UP TO FUCKING ARMED GUARDS AND ASK PERMISSION TO MURDER THEIR EMPLOYER!

LET'S CHILL, WE'RE NOT--
WHEN WERE WE TOLD TO MURDER THIS GUY?
HUH? WHEN?

FUCKING HARD-ASS COMMANDO. YOU'VE NEVER KILLED ANYONE.
SAT IN CUBA FOR TWENTY-FIVE YEARS, TRAINING FOR MISSIONS ASSIGNED BY PEOPLE YOU'VE NEVER MET FOR A PLACE YOU'VE NEVER BEEN.

BULLSHIT.

IT CHANGES YOU, ALEK.
KILLING TAKES YOUR SOUL.

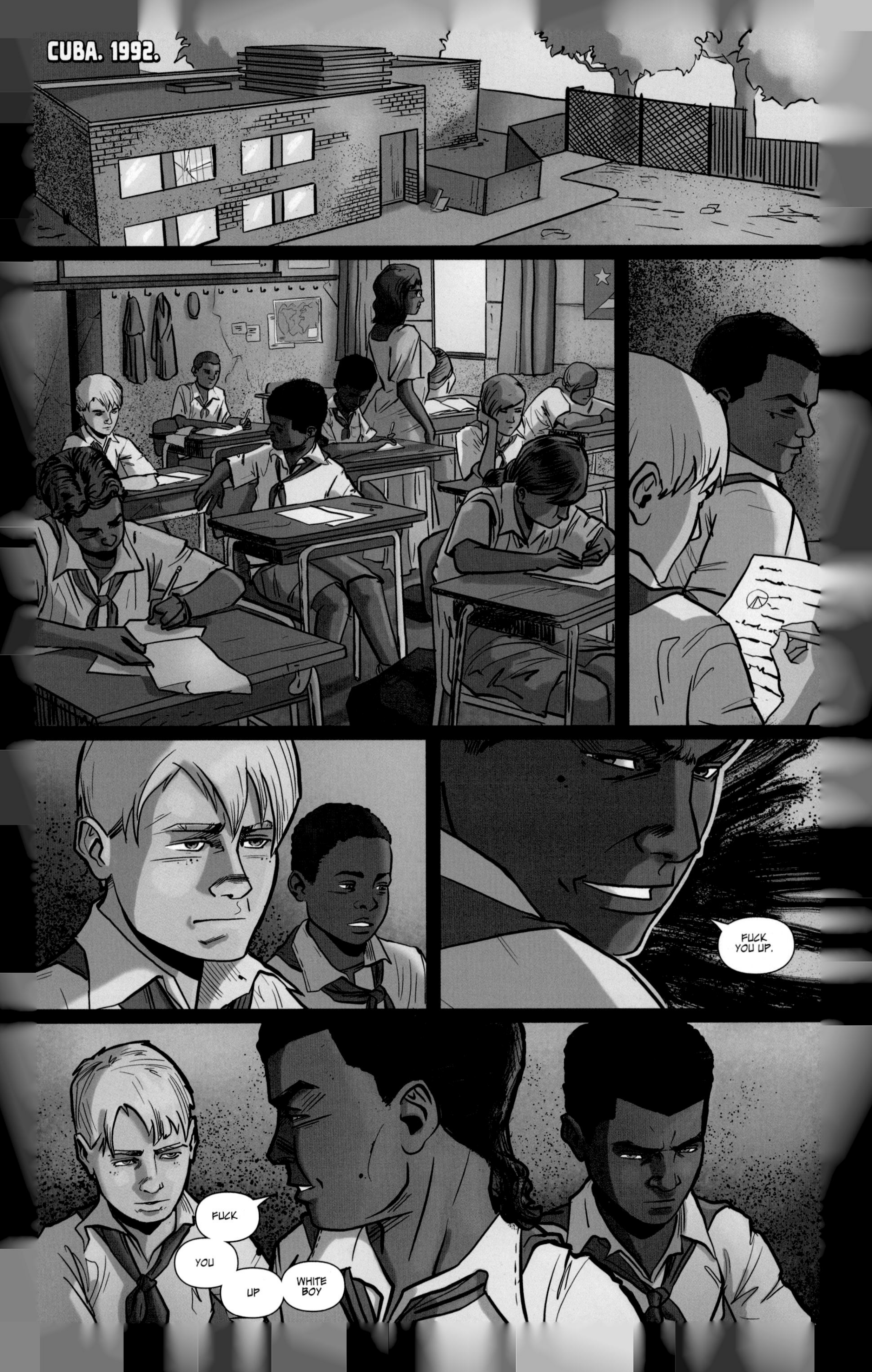
CUBA. 1992.
FUCK YOU UP.
FUCK
YOU
UP
WHITE BOY

OH, WHITE BOY.
THANK YOU FOR MAKING THIS SO EASY.
NO.
THANK YOU.
ALEK?

WH--
HUUUUUUU
AACKH
AH-HUH

MMMMT!
NO!
HUH
HUCH
CUUU
PLEASE
PLEASE
FELIX
DON'T
NNNNOOOAAAAAAAAAAAAAAAAAA

NLAAAAAAA
DON'T YOU FUCKING DARE.
MOVE.
HE'S DOING HIS JOB.

I'D LIKE A STATUS UPDATE.
ON HIS FUCKING PROGRESS.

DUM DUM
YEAH?
COME OUT.

WHAT'S UP?

THE WHITE RUSSIAN IS ASKING FOR AN UPDATE ON YOUR PROGRESS.
WELL...
I'M *TALKING.*
BUT I DON'T THINK HE'S *LISTENING.*

WHAT THE FUCK ARE YOU DOING?

HE BLEEDS 'TIL HE TALKS.
I'LL MAKE HIM TALK.

HOW? YOU GONNA GIVE HIM CANDY?

TEN MORE MINUTES SHOULD DO IT.

THEN, BY ALL MEANS...

I AM TRAINING SOLDIERS.
I AM NOT TRAINING SCHOOLYARD BULLIES.
YES, SIR.
YES, SIR.
NO. NOT FUCKING "YES, SIR." IF IT WAS "YES SIR" WE WOULDN'T BE IN THE FUCKING SITUATION WE'RE IN NOW.
WE ARE HERE IN FUCKING SECRET.
WHAT IS COVERT ABOUT A PAIR OF FUCKING TWELVE-YEAR-OLD COMMANDOS BEATING THE SHIT OUT OF THREE CUBAN BOYS IN BROAD FUCKING DAYLIGHT?
SIX.
SIXTEEN.

OLEG.
SIX.
SIXTEEN.

ROCKY.
SENATOR ROCKY.
ROCKY, I AM FROM CUBA. BUT I WORK FOR THE KGB.
WHAT... LISTEN, THIS IS ABOUT--
YOU KNOW WHAT THIS IS ABOUT. AND YOU WANNA KNOW A SECRET?
I KNOW WHAT IT'S ABOUT, TOO.
NOBODY IN THE OTHER ROOM KNOWS. THEY THINK WE'RE ON A BLIND MISSION TO GET SOME NUMBERS FROM YOU.
BUT I KNOW WHAT YOU DID.
AND I KNOW ABOUT THE LITTLE BOY.
JOSEPH, RIGHT? YOU CALL HIM JOE FOR SHORT? JOEY?
OH, GOD...

HEY, LOVE IS LOVE. I'M NOT JUDGING.

BUT IF YOU *DON'T* GIVE ME THE NUMBERS?

WHAT I DO TO YOU'LL BE TWICE AS BAD AS WHAT YOU DID TO JOEY.

IN KANSAS CITY, AT THE GUN STORE. WHEN YOU SAID "*IT WENT FINE.*"

THE SHOPKEEPER...
I LEFT HIM ALIVE.

THIS ISN'T--
IF YOU DON'T WANT IT. IF YOU DON'T HAVE THE STOMACH FOR IT ANYMORE... THEN DESERT. YOU NEED TO RUN AWAY.
BUT, DUDE. IF YOU STAY?
YOU GOTTA STOP BEING SUCH A ***PUSSY.***

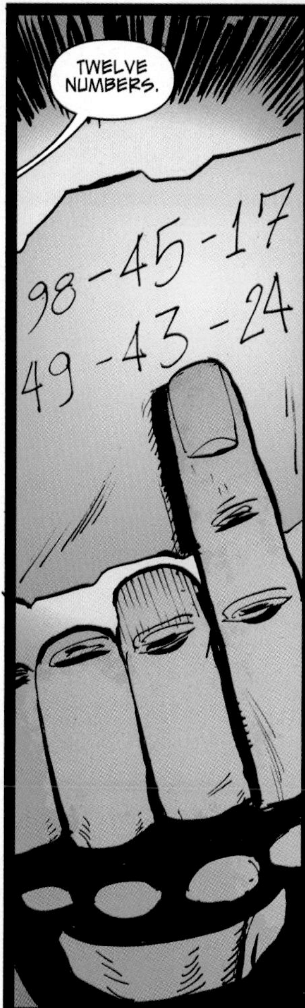
TWELVE NUMBERS.
98-45-17
49-43-24

THIS THING CAME IN HANDY, FELIX. IN A SCIENCE EXPERIMENT SORT OF WAY.

A TRANQUILIZER DART WON'T KILL YOU...

BUT SIXTEEN?
SIXTEEN WILL KILL YOU JUST FINE.
NO...

NO--

WASHINGTON, D.C.
SOON.
...WHERE THE FUCK IS THE REST OF THE PRESIDENT!?

TALK, BITCH!

I BELIEVE I ASKED FOR TEA.

OUT.
ENOUGH. OUT.

BE BACK IN A BIT.
WITH TEA.

FUCK, MAN.
HARD-ASS BITCH.
UH... SORRY, MA'AM.
THIS HAS GOTTA HURRY UP.

IF SHE'S NOT SPILLING AFTER A FUCKING BLOODY HAND'S THROWN IN HER FACE, NOTHING'S LIGHTING A FIRE UNDER HER ASS.

SHIT.

WHAT DO YOU WANT US TO DO, DIRECTOR?

DIRECTOR DAMPEER?

WE ONLY HAVE ENGLISH BREAKFAST.
MY FAVORITE.
I'M DORIS.
MAY I CALL YOU IRISA?
OF COURSE.

CAN THIS BE SOMEWHERE ELSE?

HAVANA MACHIN.
FELIX BOTKINA. AKA FELIX VASQUEZ.
ALEKSANDR WOLKOWICZ.
EKATARINA MACHIN.
VIKTOR SKIPETROVA.
TELL ME, IRISA...

WOULD YOU LIKE TO KNOW WHICH ONE DIED FIRST?
CONTINUED.

SKETCHBOOK
FELIX
HAVANA
VIKTOR
VLADIMIR
ALEXSANDR
1980
2011